Shades of the Same Skin

Creative Talents Unleashed

GENERAL INFORMATION

Shades of the Same Skin

By

Creative Talents Unleashed

1st Edition: 2016

This Publishing is protected under Copyright Law as a "Collection". All rights for all submissions are retained by the Individual Author and or Artist. No part of this publishing may be Reproduced, Transferred in any manner without the prior **WRITTEN CONSENT** of the "Material Owner" or it's Representative Creative Talents Unleashed.

www.ctupublishinggroup.com

Publisher Information
1st Edition: Creative Talents Unleashed
CreativeTalentsUnleashed@aol.com

This Collection is protected under U.S. and International Copyright laws

Copyright © 2016: Creative Talents Unleashed

ISBN-13: 978-0692679876 (Creative Talents Unleashed)
ISBN-10: 0692679871

$13.95

Credits

Book Cover

Donna J. Sanders

Editor

Donna J. Sanders

Foreword

Donna J. Sanders

Publisher

Creative Talents Unleashed

Foreword

*T*he bell pepper is a fascinating species to watch as it grows. In its youth, the green bell pepper is harvested before it begins maturity. It has a distinct bitter flavor that works best in a savory chili. In the mid-stages, yellow and orange peppers are picked but are not as popular as the green variety. With a fruity taste, these colors are better in salads or kebabs. In the final stage of maturity, the pepper turns red. It is sweeter than its predecessors and used to create pimento and paprika spices. One tree produces the same pepper in a variety of shades, giving us an assortment of flavors.

*H*umans are no different than the bell pepper. We are shades of the same skin, filled with flavors that enhance the diversity of the planet. Each generation blossoms with something new to pass down to the next and it is how we have a melting pot of culture. We have been grafted and blended over and over again; sometimes it is not that easy to trace our ancestral roots. But the heritage that runs in our veins is what makes us who we are. We take what has been passed on and fuse it with new traditions and ideas, adding essence to the cauldron of humanity.

*L*ately, it seems as if the stew has become too bitter. The world is in need of a vigorous seasoning and it is why the poets in this book are willing to share their ethnicity. Each one will give some insight into their culture, music, clothing, food, traditions, and even share a few recipes. Some will engage in unique stories and folklore. Others will take us back to their childhood days and compare it to the experience of children today. A few will even welcome us into their homes to share items from their heritage.

*T*his is also a book of unity. Its purpose is to show that without diversity, the world would be a very boring place. The bell pepper has kin from the mild to the hottest variety in so many shapes and sizes. Each one has a specific use and our dishes would suffer without them. Each poet in this anthology has a unique style because of where they came from, their experiences, and who they are. Their words are printed on these pages to inspire why we belong. We are all vital ingredients for the recipe to keep the world stirring.

Donna J. Sanders

"We are the world"

Table of Contents

Foreword	v

AROUND THE WORLD

Mexico

About the Author - Catherine Ghosh	3
Short Story – Partying with the Dead	4
Cultural photo	7
Recipe – Pan de Muerto	8

Greece

About the Author - Gust Dimoulias	10
Short Story – Greek Easter	11
Short Story – Christmas	13
Cultural photo	15

China

About the Author - Ellen Zhang	17
Poem – Tang Yuan	19
Poem – Shi Pu	20
Recipe – Four Happiness: Vegetable	21

Africa

About the Author – Donovan Beukes	24
Short Story – Rainbow Child	25
Poem – City of Good Hope	26
Recipe – Charmaine's Cape Tomato Bredie (Stew)	28
About the Author – Sue Lobo	29
Short Story – Special Friends	30

Table of Contents . . . continued

Poem – River Deep Secret   32
Cultural Photo   33

India

About the Author – Vincent Van Ross   35
Poem – Unity in Diversity   37
Poem – Indian at Heart   38
Recipe – Rava Upma   39

Italy

About the Author – Joan Leotta   41
Short Story – The Oak Table Discussion   43
Poem – On the Making of Pizzelle   45
Recipe – Eggplant Parmesan   46

England

About the Author – Laura Marie Clark   48
Short Story – Almost an Egyptian Bride   49
Poem – The Lincoln Imp   50
Cultural Photo   51

About the Author – Lynn White   52
Poem – Ripples   53
Poem – A Grey Place?   54

CARIBBEAN ISLANDS

Puerto Rico

About the Author – Shirley Ann Cooper   57

Table of Contents . . . continued

Short Story – My Island, Beautiful	59
Poem – El Yunque Intertwined With My Heart	60
Recipe – Red & Pink Beans	61

Jamaica

About the Author – Christena AV Williams	64
Poem – Out of Many, One People	65
Poem – The Great Reggae Legend	67
Recipe – Mango Smoothie	68

Trinidad & Tobago

About the Author – Donna J. Sanders	70
Poem – Pelau	72
Cultural Photo	73
Recipe – Green Seasoning	74

USA

Michigan

About the Author – Ryan Vallee	77
Poem – The Boy Who Buried His Dog in the Sand	78
Cultural Photo	79

New York

About the Author – Nolan P. Holloway	81
Poem – Outer Layer	82
Poem – Face of the Mandrill	83
Cultural Photo	84

North Carolina

About the Author – David Hall	86

Table of Contents . . . continued

Short Story – The Bent Tree	87
Poem – Of the Past and Now	89
About the Author – Rusty Shuping	90
Short Story – Morning Word	91
Short Story – The Shop	92
Poem – Sandpiper	93

Oregon

About the Author – Adam Brown	95
Short Story – The Slug	96
Poem – California Fun	97
Cultural Photo	98

Epilogue

The Starving Artist Fund	100
Our Links	101
Book Credits	102

Shades of the Same Skin

Creative Talents Unleashed

AROUND THE WORLD

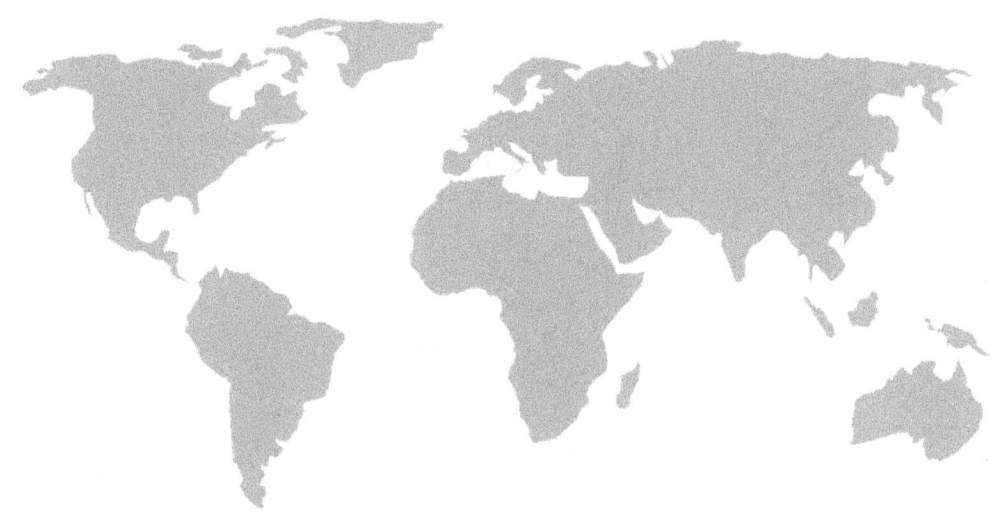

Mexico

Shades of the Same Skin

Catherine Ghosh

From: Mexico
Currently resides: Virginia, USA

I have always been very sensitive to the world around me. I grew up in a valley surrounded by live volcanoes, in a city that was built upon a lake. At the very center of the city, called the Zócalo, there are buildings that tilt because of this.

Mexico City was built in such a seemingly precarious location, because of an Aztec King who believed in omens. Legend tells that the king instructed the people to settle only where they saw a heavenly eagle, with a snake in his mouth, sitting atop a cactus. The faithful people lived as nomads for years, until this very image appeared before them. Disregarding the fact that the omen had been spotted on a little island, in the middle of a lake, surrounded by active volcanoes—loyal to the king's sacred vision—the people built their city atop the lake, in defiance to all those who said their endeavors would prove useless.

The city has now become one of the most densely populated in the world! I've always been inspired by this Mexican geography of my childhood because, to me, it represents having faith, taking risks and emerging triumphant against all odds. Mexico is therefore a city of joyful and colorful festivals that seem to declare: "What seems impossible becomes possible!"

Even as a child, I saw this hope in the smiles of the Mexican people. When I was 12 and my family moved out of Mexico City, I felt like a plant that had been uprooted from her nourishing soil and plopped into the desert of Southern California. For the Mexican legends and lifestyle had inevitably been woven into the emotional tapestry of who I was then, and who I am still, today.

Though I live in Virginia now, I carry the magnificent valley of Mexico City in my heart, complete with her majestic views of live volcanoes, and the notion that nothing is impossible if you set your heart on it. I like to believe that that this message trickles into everything I write.

Catherine's page: http://www.catherineghosh.com

Partying with the Dead

The year I turned eight, I waited for my deceased friend, Monica, to return from the dead to play a game of tetherball with me. I wanted to meet with her under the streetlight outside our homes, like we used to when she was alive. I waited and waited, until I was called inside. That night, before I fell asleep, I thought I heard her voice softly trickling in through the bedroom wall we shared.

For, in the land I was raised, we invite the deceased to move among us once a year, on the day known as *Dia de Los Muertos*, or The Day of The Dead. As a child growing up in Mexico, it was never too clear to me if the dead came back to life for this festival, or if we, the living, became temporarily dead. For the rituals included decorating the foreheads of sugar skulls and tombstones with our own names, as we playfully blurred the lines between where life ended and where death began.

I have fond memories of walking under lines of delicate paper flags flapping in the chilly, autumn wind, as colorful reminders of the fragile threshold that divides this world from the afterlife. The sound they made was said to hide the whispers of the deceased calling out to us. These bright pink, orange and purple flags made of *papel picado* were usually decorated with skeletons, carefully chiseled into the tissue paper, bearing phrases that celebrated our immortality like *Amor Eterno* or "Eternal Love". For love, we were taught, is stronger than death. And this love would serve as the vehicle connecting the two realms, widely opening the gates that normally separate them. This excited me to no end!

The first to attend the Party of the Dead, are the deceased children, for the strongest lures are made of a mother's love. Beginning at midnight, on October 31st it is believed that families are reunited for 24 hours with children they had lost. Over the next two days, November first and second, the child-spirits are followed by the spirits of the deceased adults, which are summoned with the help of elaborate altars meant to lure all their senses. These never failed to capture mine as well!

I will always be haunted by the delicious scent of anise baked into the *Pan de los Muertos*, or "Bread of the Dead": sweet loafs whose dough is shaped to look like bones. Some were braided into circles to represent the cycle of life and death, or decorated with sugary teardrops as a way to sweeten the sorrow of grief. I always loved accompanying my mother to the bakery on Mexican festival days.

Shades of the Same Skin

And I remember the strong women who carried oversized bushels of freshly picked *cempasuchil,* or wild marigolds in their shawls, while balancing toddlers on their hips. Like their Aztec ancestors, they had faith that the bright, orange blossoms would draw in the dead with their strong scent. For these flowers had healing properties that, traditionally, could have only come from the powerful afterlife.

From our rooftop, I watched the hills of San Bernabé flicker with candlelight as the graveyards swelled with anticipation and excitement. Every tombstone was adorned in ways that would help guide the spirits back. The offerings would include the deceased favorite dishes, incense, and live music, as the dead became guests of honor at the party. Altars of offerings were built in seven levels representing the universal elements the soul had to traverse to reach the afterlife. Above each altar is a large arch made of flowers. It represents the river believed to divide the temporary realm of existence from the eternal one.

Aztec mythology depicted this river as a stream of blood in which fearsome jaguars swam. Once a year, on The Day of The Dead, the river turns to flowers, making it effortless to cross. I spent a good portion of my childhood curiously searching for this river: looking for easy entrances into whatever existed beyond death, longing for answers to one of life's greatest mysteries. The books in my father's library gave me a plethora of perspectives, some more memorable than others.

Unforgettable is the day I stumbled upon glossy images of Michelangelo's Last Judgment, complete with apocalyptic angels waking the dead with trumpets, the naked Greek God of the underworld wrapped in a black serpent, devils escorting souls to hell, and especially the tortured expressions on the faces of their dead, terrified passengers. At eight, I definitely preferred the smiley faces of the skeletons that danced around Mexico on *Dia De Los Muertos.* And where were all the women in this painting?

Unlike the Greek, Hindu, Buddhist and Egyptian cultures, which depict the god of death as male, the Day of The Dead is presided over by a female goddess known as Mictecacihuatl, or "The Lady of The Dead". It is she who grants the passage to infinite life, and this time of year, Mexico City explodes in her colorful, skeletal effigies. Along with fanciful paper maché skeletons that appear to be enjoying themselves, "The Lady of The Dead" is found around every corner, in the decorations around the city, and as the citizens of Mexico themselves, who dawn her disguise, making it impossible to tell who the real Mictecacihuatl is!

It is believed that on The Day of The Dead you never know if the people you run into on the street are dead or alive, and that all the graveyards overflow with partying spirits. To this day, graveyards excite me. They trace flickering lines between the animated bones in my body and the ones that decompose under the earth, inside coffins. They remind me that my stay here is limited and that the time of my exit is a complete and absolute mystery. I see my name carved into the tombstones and it doesn't terrify me.

Every autumn I feel old parts of myself, and my life, dying. Sometimes I don't realize this until struck by the sudden grief that comes with the prospect of burying them. I float through the catacombs of my consciousness taking inventory of expired wounds from my past, and of those that still haunt me; ones I'd like to descend on like frost sucks the green out of grass on cold mornings, or the Lady of The Dead sucks the life out of the dying. For, *death means progress*, she says. Death indicates dynamic evolution. Death is the shadow cast by the light of life itself. In Mexico, we party with the dead once a year. Ironically, it's my favorite celebration of life!

Shades of the Same Skin

Cultural Photo

Catherine Ghosh dressed up for a Day of the Dead party

Pan de Muerto (Bread of the Dead –vegan version)

Ingredients:

1/4 cup unsweetened almond milk
¼ cup coconut butter
¼ cup sugar
½ tsp salt
1 package of active, dry yeast
¼ cup very warm water
3 cup all-purpose flour
½ tsp anise seed
¼ tsp ground cinnamon
2 Tbsp. sugar
2 Tbsp. egg-replacer

Directions:

1. Bring almond milk to boil and remove from heat
2. Stir in coconut butter, ¼ c sugar and salt
3. In large bowl mix yeast with warm water until dissolved and let stand 5 min.
4. Add almond milk mixture
5. Add 1 T egg replacer to the yeast mix, followed by the flour
6. Blend well to form dough ball
7. Knead dough until smooth
8. Return to large bowl and cover with damp towel. Let rise for 90 min.
9. Preheat oven to 350 degrees
10. Knead dough again on floured surface
11. Divide dough into 4ths and set aside one forth
12. Roll the remaining 3 pieces of dough into three ropes
13. On greased baking sheet pinch three ropes together at top& braid them
14. Divide remaining forth of dough into two and make two "bone shapes"
15. Lay the "bones" on top of the braided dough
16. Cover dough with dishtowel and let rise 30 min.
17. In a sauce pan mix anise seed, cinnamon, and 2 T sugar
18. Cook down until sugar melts
19. After the dough has risen for 30 min. brush the sugar mixture on it
20. Bake at 350 degrees for 35 minutes

Shades of the Same Skin

Greece

Gust Dimoulias

Ancestry: Greece
Currently resides: Illinois, USA

My name is Gust Dimoulias and I am from the City of Chicago and the State of Illinois. My ancestry on my father's side is from Greece - a small village near the Ionian Sea. On my mother's side is Greek and Irish. My maternal grandmother was Irish but my maternal grandfather, who I am named from, was Greek.

I never learned much about the Irish part of my family. We were Greek. I learned to speak and read Greek and was raised in the Greek Orthodox Church. Over the course of forty years I learned what it meant to be Greek. Our culture goes back over centuries and in to the ancient world. Sadness, joy, love, and loss are all heard in our poetry, short stories, or novels.

My past is reflected in my writing. In my writing my constant readers get a view of my experiences which are colored by my culture. The main character of my stories is a bit of me, and a bit of my father. The character's experiences are my experiences. Secondary characters incorporate other people that have flitted in and out of my life.

Join me in the next three pages while I tell you a little more about your humble scribe. I'll tell you a couple of stories from my childhood; traditions from my culture with a little familial twist. My most fervent hope is that what you read will resonate on some level within each of you constant readers.

Greek Easter

In the life of every family of Greek decent the church is at the center. One of the truly clear memories I have is the celebration of Easter. The United States celebrates Easter with the Easter Bunny and chocolate eggs and hard boiled eggs painted in bright colors. Countries who practice the Orthodox Faith celebrate Easter in their own way coloring their eggs differently. My family celebrated in their own way.

When I was young my family was very traditional. Dad was the head of the household, and while my brother and I were branches, my mother was the heart and spirit. It was she that kept the traditions of our Orthodox Faith and family. The true celebration began months earlier with The Great Lent.

Great Lent is a forty day period of fasting that prepares the faithful for Easter Sunday. Lent always meant going to church every Friday and Sunday to venerate Saints, The Virgin Mary, and Orthodoxy. Our family always fasted heavily in the first week of Great Lent. Every week brought us closer to Holy Week.

Our preparation for Holy Week always started with dad going to a Greek butcher and buying a whole lamb. When I say a whole lamb, I mean with the head, hoofs, and everything. One year I told dad I don't think I could eat anything that could look back at me. We cut up the beast in to parts and stored them in the refrigerator until our Easter dinner. Dad also kept the entrails and the heart and the liver.

Holy Week began with Palm Sunday and ended with Easter Sunday. Each day commemorated a Saint or an event of Jesus' last week on earth. Each day was a church service. On Holy Wednesday we celebrated the Sacrament of Holy Unction. Holy Thursday we commemorated Jesus' passion and death. At home mom always spent the day dyeing eggs red.

Good Friday services lasted all day. The priest would read the hours of Christ's passion. In the midafternoon we commemorated Jesus being taken down from His cross. In the evening we all went to church to chant the Lamentations, which are a funerary dirge. Easter, or Resurrection services started on Saturday night.

The Resurrection services would go all night and we would not get home until three in the morning. We cracked an egg between ourselves, which was a game; the one whose egg remained whole won the game. Mom would cook lamb and a soup called *magiritsa*, which is made from the intestines, heart, and liver of the lamb. We carried the light of the Resurrection for forty days.

Christmas

The Christmas season was always a time of magic and mystery. It always seemed easy for others to celebrate Christmas in the commercial way. We could buy a tree, decorate it, buy gifts, and open them Christmas morning. But in Greece, Christmas, like Easter, is centered on the church. We never celebrated Christmas in exactly the way they do in Greece.

The Christmas season would begin with a Lenten period most commonly called Advent. Fasting and going to church where hymns were chanted to the pre-eternal Christ. We wouldn't buy the tree after Thanksgiving the way many do. We always waited a week or two before Christmas to buy the tree.

We decorated the tree with gold and silver tinsel. Covered the tree with multi-colored lights that flashed. Placed ornaments that were kept from when I was in Grammar School. Once the tree was sufficiently decorated I would perform a certain ritual. I had to close every light in the house so I could watch the tree. Mom always laughed as I continued this ritual even in my teenage years. I think she still laughs even though she is gone and continue the ritual.

In Greece, the children in the little villages would go door to door singing local Christmas carols. If the singing was any good, the children would be given sweet treats. Such a tradition is impossible to do here in Chicago. Instead of going door to door we sung Christmas carols with our church's choir. We weren't given sweet treats, but my mother's smile was more than enough to make singing with the adults worthwhile.

Christmas Eve is normally spent in church for a midnight liturgical service. My father taught me that Christmas was not about Santa Claus or presents. Dad taught me Christmas was about the ultimate gift of Jesus Christ being born. Greeks didn't have Santa Claus, we have Saint Basil. Gifts are exchanged on the Day of the Epiphany.

Mom had always gotten dress shirts for us and she would let us open those gifts. The dress shirts were to be worn for church on Christmas Day. Mom always fawned over us in our suits. She never went to church with us as Mom needed to stay home to cook. As any son will tell you there is nothing so good as your mother's cooking.

Shades of the Same Skin

On the Feast of the Epiphany dad would cut a bough from our Christmas tree. We would bless our dwelling by dipping the bough in to a pot of Holy Water and spray them everywhere. Dad or I would chant the hymn of the day "In the Jordan were you baptized Oh Lord." This would be done in every room of our house. Once the house was blessed we would take the tree down and dump it off so that it could be put in a wood chipper.

Shades of the Same Skin

Cultural Photo

This is a photo of what called a εικονοστάσιο in Greek or an Icon Screen in English. In many Greek homes this is placed on a wall or a niche in a wall. The family members will venerate the icons before meals or going to bed. To the Orthodox Christian the icons are windows in to heaven. The church is the central pillar of our lives.

For me these Icons are tied to my past. I say my past, but I do not mean my own direct past. The past I speak of is my ancestral past -those Greeks who venerated similar Icons such as the ones pictured and chanted the same hymns that I chant when I am at church. These Icons tie me to those people as with ropes.

Shades of the Same Skin

China

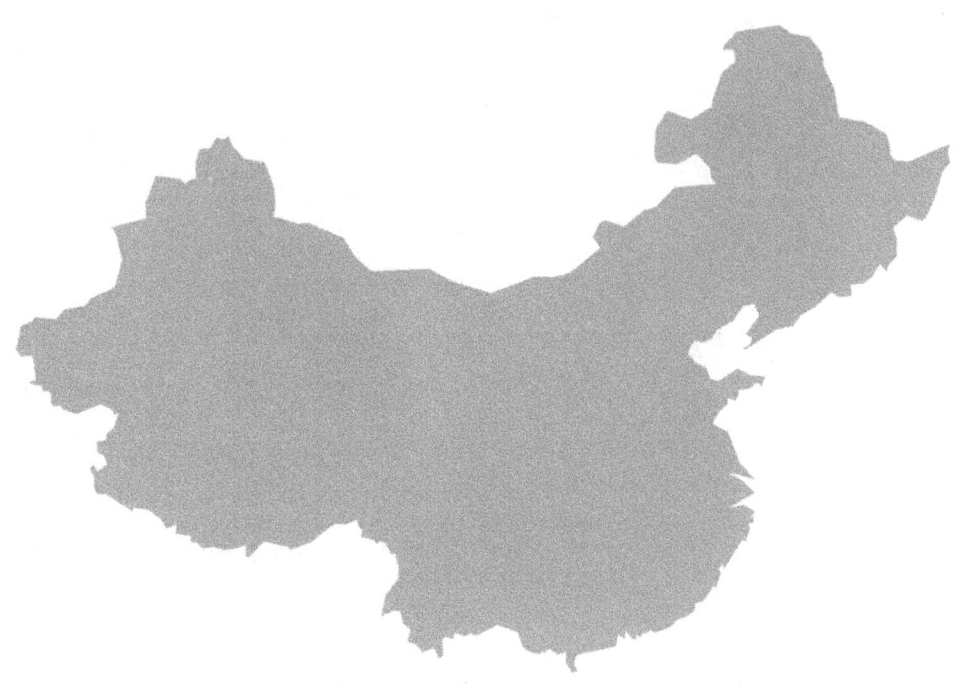

Ellen Zhang

Ancestry: China
Currently resides: Massachusetts, USA

Ellen Zhang is an Asian-American studying and living Cambridge, Massachusetts. She is incredibly grateful and in awe of her parent's sacrifices of immigrating to a new country with little in their pockets and big dreams—an experience that has transformed her life unlike any other.

The very dichotomy of being American and Chinese—growing up as an American Born Chinese—has shaped Ellen into the person she is today. The two cultures inevitably melt and blend together to produce something new and exciting. Personally, Ellen has kept her heritage alive through speaking mandarin fluently, volunteering at her local cultural center, visiting relatives in China, and through Chinese cuisine.

Ellen is reminded of her heritage and its importance daily with each mouthful of food she intakes. One sip of warm lamb stew transports her back to Xianjiang, her parents' homeland. A small morsel of *nian gao* brings back memories of her grandmother's hands sticky with rice. In her kitchen, there is a sweet scent of both eastern and western culture.

Outside of the kitchen, Ellen explores her rich cultural heritage through writing; Amy Tan and Margaret Cho are her inspirations for they are able to masterfully intertwine their culture within their works to create something new and exciting. She is also inspired by Detroit's most recent venture, "Write a House," which renovates run-down homes with crumbling ceilings and holes in walls, to bring in writers to contribute to the local literary community. The goal of this project is to use creativity to create hope and a bright vision of the future. With her ideas, imagination, experiences, and a pen in her hand, she, too, want to create possibilities.

Ultimately, writing, for Ellen, is a kaleidoscope lens to integrate the shards of her experiences, thoughts, and observations into a beautiful gestalt and she wants to use it as a medium to spread her thoughts, ideas, and unique experiences. Her works center on culture experiences such as the Chinese

Lantern Festival, or simple things, like her mother's appetizing dumplings.

At fifteen, Ellen wanted to give back to her Chinese Culture Center which has not only connected her more to her roots, but has also given her a strong sense of community. After presenting her idea to a committee, Ellen started a Creative Writing class. She sees her younger self, curious and inquisitive, manifested the elementary schoolers as they discovered the power of words. Ultimately, her fascination with her background leads her to investigate Chinese current affairs and works of Asian-American writers such as Laurence Yep and Li-Young Lee. Ellen's cultural identity is as much as something she was born with, as it is her personal choice.

Tang Yuan

My *nainai,* grandmother, kneads dough and
it is difficult to tell where epidermis and
flour separate. She chides me gently while
I help her make *Tang Yuan.* The white powder as
blinding as her silky hair. Her eyes laugh as she tells me
of the lanterns that will come this *Yuan Xiao.* Already,
the images of lights, fireworks, and laughter consume me,
we tease each other with smiles. Her calloused hands
gently caressing mine; scooping bean paste into
our balls of hope. "This is how we pray" she whispers.
and I giggle, as if in understanding.

Plop and in drop the sweet balls. Lips watering in
anticipation. Already, I can smell the hot, steamy aroma.
Nainai tells me how *Tang Yuan* are made
like pearls are formed from a grain of sand with love,
dedication. Plop, plop. Sound echoing, vibrating,
echoing like the rain that washed away every last lantern
and lullabies of mandarin. Thoughts floating like calligraphy
letters, my fingertips hovering and yearning,
but there is nobody, nothing, here.
Hands shaking, making *Tang Yuan,*
praying for you to get better. But I still do not
understand, your face only a distant echo.

They do not taste as sweet, as vivid
as they used to. The laughter never as
naive. I cannot consume, will not be consumed.
This is the ending, I thought; ebony velvet dress too tight
Your hands folded across your chest; lips forever parted
But where is the epilogue? Where are my
pearls from my grains of despair?

Shi Pu

My mother's hands sweep slices
of chives with the nimble sheen of the blade,
knife cleverly kissing the cutting board.
Slowly, the pungent ginger accent is
replaced with the warm, comforting fragrance
of *he zi*, shaped like dumplings but
fried and smothered in savory sauce.
The shape, she whispers,
is for good fortune, as her palms
fold and form the dough.
Spoon dipping in and out of the filling
that sags into the shells of the *he zi,*
Her hands breathe synonym for love.

Fragments of memories are the only remains,
searching for something sentimental,
hoping that something will be enough,
dust settling on my lungs before I gaze
at familiarity in the form of a black composition notebook,
simple decisive characters, *shi pu*— recipes
I skim it only to start pouring over it,
trying to satisfy the constricting in my chest,
examining like the art of ikebana.

Some entries are copied in meticulous letters,
others cut from magazines and diligently pasted,
pictures matched neatly to each one,
cryptic comments line the margins,
as the fluttering of birds dancing upon telephone wires,
ready to take wind and fly with ease,
My hands trace over the strokes in wonder,
"Liang's favorite," "Su's dinner party"
My lips mutter sentimental, yet
my hands dice and slice vegetables.
Already, I can feel the tinge of sweet sauce on my tongue,
before my hands press and push the dough,
filling it up with good fortunate,
before I whiff the redolence of *he zi* that take me back to generations past.

Four Happiness: Vegetable

Ingredients:

1 cup vital wheat gluten
1 tea spoon yeast
1 cup warm water
¼ lb fresh snow pea
Half a head of cauliflower
¼ lb fresh mushroom
1 teaspoon soy sauce
½ teaspoon salt
1 tablespoon sugar
½ cup water
½ cup oil

Directions:

Step 1: Make the dough: in a bowl, mix together Vital wheat Gluten, yeast, and warm water. When the mixture is at a good consistency, knead the dough with hands until its surface is smooth and elastic.

Step 2: Grease a large bowl with oil and put the dough in the bowl with a clean, damp dish towel over it. Place the bowl in a warm, draft-free location — between 75 and 85 degrees Fahrenheit is ideal—until the dough has doubled in size, about 1 to and 2 hours.

Step 3: Add water in a wok, and put dough on the steam-plate. Cover wok with lid, and turn the heat on to high. Gently steam the dough over water for 15 minutes.

Step 4: Turn off the heat and wait for 20 minute before removing the lid.

Step 5: While waiting, cut the fresh mushrooms into thin, even slices and cut the cauliflowers into quarters.

Step 6: Take out the dough and cut it to 2x2 inch squares.

Step 7: Heat ½ inch of oil in a large frying pan over medium heat. Fry the dough for 1 minute on each side or until crisp and golden; then turn the heat onto high before adding fresh snow peas, prepared cauliflower and prepared, fresh mushroom. Mix everything for about 2 minutes.

Step 8: Add soy sauce, salt, and sugar; stir until evenly incorporated.

Step 9: Add ½ cup cold water and turn the heat to medium level, and boil until the water is completely evaporated. Plate, serve, and enjoy!

Shades of the Same Skin

Africa

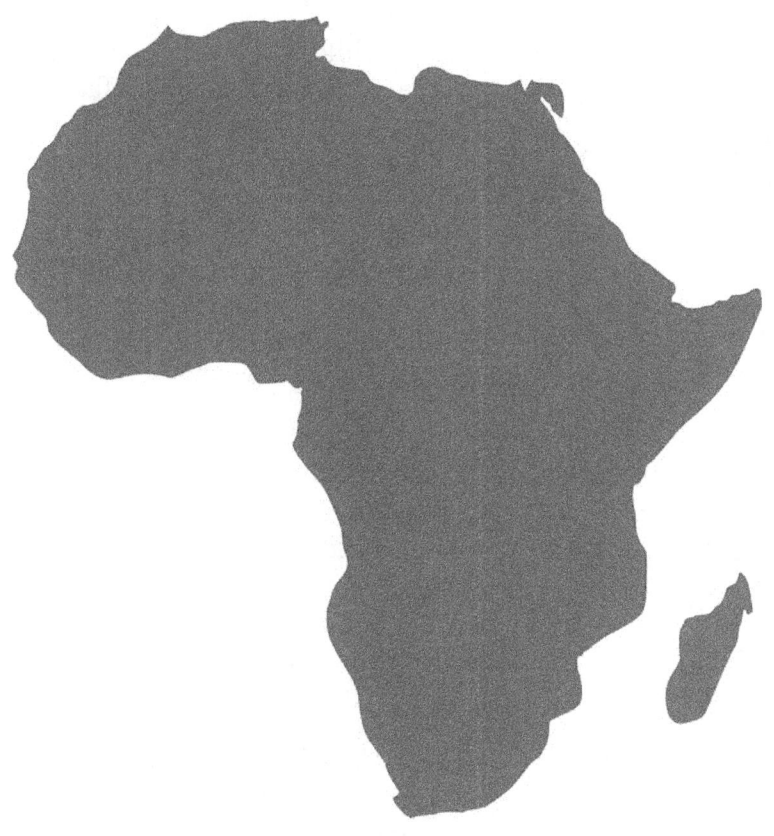

Donovan Beukes

From: Cape Town, South Africa
Currently resides: Côte D'Amor, France

I was born, raised and educated in the last two decades of Apartheid at the most southern tip of the African continent, in the city of Cape Town, South Africa.

As a 'child of colour' from mixed race heritage and a great-grandfather who was German, my family and I, along with millions of others from mixed race heritage, were lawfully identified as 'coloured' and the same for black people from a tribal cultural background and Indian people.

This meant that 'non-whites' could not choose where to live or even go to a beach of their choice around our beautiful coastline.

Despite being made invisible and made to feel as a lesser member of South African society by a divisive and racist government, I grew up in a loving Christian family home. I was given the confidence by them to achieve anything I wanted to through the power of Education and ultimately studied to be a teacher of English and Geography, which was how I ended up living in the UK in 1999, which was a memorable culture shock of depressing grey clouds and a stiff upper lip society, where foreigners were mistrusted and curiously observed.

Childhood memories include trips to the beaches around the Cape Peninsula, train journeys to the South Coast and a summer Christmas table of cold meats, mixed seafood and salads. I was also introduced to traditional Malay cuisine from our Muslim neighbours.

In the shadow of majestic Table Mountain standing guard over Cape Town, dreams were forged, dented and repaired. The cultures, languages and people shaped my individuality and prepared me for the global village I am proud to be part of, which now permeates into my writing.

Don's page : https://about.me/donbeukes

Rainbow Child

Growing up in the early seventies in Cape Town, South Africa, I had no clue that I was racially identified as coloured by the government in power and certainly did not identify myself as anything but what I felt inside of me emotionally.

The love of my family and the caring environment I existed in shaped my self-image and my own understanding of the world around me. I must unashamedly admit to you that I was hopelessly spoilt by my mother and my two older sisters, Ruth and Joan, who inspired me with their endless joy for life.

My earliest memories of feeling 'other' than what I was used to, was when I went on my first train trip into the city for a day out. I just could not understand why I was unable to play with the kids who were lighter than me in the next carriage. My questions fell on deaf ears. Later in my first restaurant experience, I asked my sister why the waitress just threw our utensils on the table and spoke so rudely to us. She just insisted I eat my seafood platter. I only noticed when we returned to the central station that all the whites went a different way.

It was only in high school on my first seaside holiday that I experienced public racism.

We camped in a 'coloured' only resort in Struisbaai on the south coast. One morning my cousins decided to venture along the bay to the whites only resort, we were met by disdainful suspicious eyes glaring at our daring excursion and prevented to go any further by burly policemen and an old lady shaking her fists at us.

The scene was so bizarre we burst out laughing and shouted back in Afrikaans with our own expletives.

City of Good Hope

Rising from the tip of
a mighty continent
centurion defender and
surely divine sent -
Tafelberg still guards
over Cape Town city
our mother city
of good hope
millenia old lashed by
Atlantic raging forces
Poseidon's watery fortress -
Liquid contortions
colonial misfortunes
shaming Khoi daughters -
European invasion
natural beauty sensation
Dutch fortification linguistic
raping – Forced cultural reaping
shaping subsequent generational
hating – New permanent order
insatiable new world greed leading to
cultural murder – A new nation forged
from forced integration
lucrative marine ocean basket
hiding the colonial cocooned casket -
Mother City of four hundred years
still harbouring underlying familiar fears

A new democratic political order
shunning old racist fodder
citizens apparently united despite
current discontent sighted -
A city pulsating
existing opportunities inciting
heroes in the making – Its heart
still unknown
new generational groan
still battling to culturally cope

in our mother city of good hope.

> **Tafelberg** – Afrikaans (One of 11 official South African languages) for Table Mountain, the iconic new Natural Wonder of the world rising over 1000 m above the city of Cape Town
>
> **Khoi** – Original beach-dwelling tribe who met the first Dutch colonists in 1652 when Jan Van Riebeeck set up a fort as a stop-over for voyagers along the spice route to the far east

Charmaine's Cape Tomato *Bredie* (Stew)

Ingredients:

1 large onion (peeled and chopped)
800 gram lamb or mutton pieces
2 stick cinnamon
4 fresh tomatoes
1 teaspoon mixed herbs
500 gram garlic and basil pasta sauce
4 – 5 potatoes (cut in equal pieces of 4 depending on the size of each potato)
salt and pepper
1 tablespoon bicarb of soda
1 tablespoon crushed garlic
basmati rice or couscous
750 ml water (to cover onions and meat)
500 ml water (to cover the rest of the cooking)

Optional ingredients:

alternative sauce containing garlic and basil as main ingredients (if pasta sauce not available)
fresh mixed herbs

Directions:

- Place chopped onion and meat into pot and cover with 750ml water. Bring to boil for 45 minutes.
- Do not let pot get dry. Add more water if it does.
- Add chopped tomatoes with 500 ml water and cook until meat is soft.
- Add crushed garlic, mixed herbs and potatoes and cook until potatoes are soft.
- Add pasta sauce and salt and pepper to taste.
- Cook for another 5 minutes.
- Add bicarb of soda and cook for a further 10 minutes.
- Serve with basmati rice or couscous.

Sue Lobo

Lived in: Botswana, Africa
Current resides: Spain

Sue Lobo is the author of three books of her experiences in Africa, a poetry book "Africa My Africa" which is poetry reflecting African life in the terrible apartheid era in South Africa & "Lollipops of Dust", her autobiography, of a child's view of living in colonial Africa, in the Kalahari desert, with all the magic of what the old Africa had to offer.

Her last book "The Last Dance" was published by Creative talents Unleashed. She has also participated in eleven poetry anthologies with other very talented poets & has won a couple poetry competitions in Gibraltar & Spain.

On occasions she has written requested epitaphs and elegies for families of departed souls. She is married to a Spaniard, with two grown up sons & presently lives in Spain.

Sue's page: www.ctupublishinggroup.com/sue-lobo.html

Special Friends

It was the early 1950's, The Bechuanaland Protectorate, now known as Botswana. It was still a British colony & my father was sent out as District Commissioner (D.C). Every two years we were sent to another station so we lived all over the country. We had been in one station for a couple of years & now we were in the new place & getting used to the rural surroundings, no neighbours, no proper running water, no electricity, no TV, no radio, no shops, nothing. But we lived on the banks of the river & the hippos would wend their way into our garden at night to eat all our vegetables, elephants, lion, leopards, snakes & myriads of different animals were my only friends & I loved it.

My first little school was in the trunk of a big baobab tree with all the little black children & it was the only school I ever loved. I was only three years old at the time, already forgetting English & spoke Setswana perfectly. My parents thought I was a savage, but oh I was so free. My nanny Aggie, whom I adored, would dress me in the morning but I would strip off to my pants & go off barefooted into the bush.

There was one thing that worried me though & that was when I lay in bed at night I heard drums from across the river & I thought they were cannibals or other scary things that kids have in their imaginations, so I decided to look for the drummers & ask them to please stop because I couldn't sleep at night, oh for the innocent naivety of children.

So one day I went down to the river bank where the fishermen kept their mokoros (dug- out tree- trunk canoes.) There were two there that day, & although I was only three, I was a fat sturdy, nut brown little girl. I pushed the canoe into the water, got in & with the pole I poled myself across the crocodile & hippo laden water. It was a hot day, the only sounds were of the bush & I was on a mission.

On getting to the other side & pulling the raft up onto the bank, I set off into the bush. I was about to give up & turn back as now I was feeling a little afraid, when I heard voices, so I continued & didn't have to go far when I came across a clearing & a group of little golden people that I had not seen before. On seeing me they whooped, chatted, clicked, laughed & danced. I just stood there with my finger in my mouth while they surrounded me & started poking me, opening my mouth, pulling at my pants elastic, fiddling with my hair & all the while in a twitter of excitement.

Shades of the Same Skin

An old woman in the group pulled me to a log & gestured that I sit on it & another brought me a gourde with a gooey golden stuff with locusts & other insects floating on the top (protein) & they gestured that I drink it which I did & it was a delicious wild honey & the crunchy insects were yummy too. (Living in the bush, everything was edible). Suddenly Aggie came crashing through the bush shouting like a banshee, grabbing my arm & started smacking me & telling me I was a bad girl in her language.

The Bushmen all converged on her telling her that she must never smack a child. Aggie wasn't a Bushman but she spoke their lingo so she backed off pulling me with her. The gentle golden people told Aggie that they had heard of the white people & knew they lived across the river, but they had never actually seen one because when they felt them near they went into hiding & that I was the first one they had seen.

When Aggie found me missing she had followed my footsteps in the sand & when finding the fisherman bemoaning his missing mokoro she had put two & two together & had followed me. I was taken home where Aggie told my parents what had happened & I was put to bed with no supper, but that didn't worry me as I was full with honey.

That night the drums sounded friendly & not ominous at all. The next morning when I went out to play, there was a beautiful ostrich egg on my doorstep, a gift from my new friends who rowed across the river every night after that day & left a gift each night. Beads made out of everything they could find, eggs, skins, precious stones, whatever they had. I feel truly blessed & have had many meetings with various groups since that day.

River Deep Secret

I share a river-deep secret with Africa;
We both know the reason for weeping,
It has nothing to do with being the dark continent
It has something to do with being the dark mind,
The bloody tears have flowed through dusty centuries,
And we are still so homeless.

We are as lost as the Bushman on Kruger Street,
As wet as the hippo's tears in his muddy hollow life,
As old as the echo across vacant Karoo plain,,
We are as fierce as the beast at his bloody repast,
As distant as the Botswana drum across dry river bed,
And we are still so homeless.

Our thundered sky is weary of tears,
But our dark lids are full of rain,
The black man runs, so does the cheetah,
Black has little to do with the skin,
Black is only the colour of the sad soul,
And we are still so homeless.

I share a river deep secret with Africa,
We both know the reason for weeping,
The earth cares little, the stars know,
The moon laughs hysterically at the crazed sun,
While he burns his promise, & turns us black,
And we are still so homeless.

Cultural Photo

My African Nativity carved out of soap stone & the last gift to me by my father before he passed away.

Shades of the Same Skin

India

Vincent Van Ross

Vincent Van Ross is a freelance journalist and writer. He writes on national and international politics, defense, environment, travel, art and culture, social themes, spirituality, philosophy, conservation and a whole lot of other issues.

Vincent's articles and features have appeared in The Hindustan Times, The Pioneer, The Hindu, The Tribune, The Statesman, National Herald, Sahara Time, Speaking Tree (The Times of India), Daily Excelsior, Northern India Patrika, Himachal Times, Free Press, The Free Press Journal, The Sentinel, Newstime and several other newspapers and periodicals in India. Currently, he writes a weekly column called 'Musing' for the Bangladesh Newspaper 'The Independent.'

Vincent has been on the editorial board of several small and medium publications. He is fond of writing humour. His humorous writings have been carried in the 'Morning Cup,' 'Flipside,' 'Silly Point,' 'Guest Column,' 'Musing' and middle columns of newspapers and magazines.

Apart from these, Vincent writes fiction, poetry and dabbles in creative photography. Some of his Hindi poems were included in an anthology of Hindi Poems called 'Guldasta' some 15 years ago. Many of his English poems have appeared in national and international anthologies. Several of his English poems are posted in various sites on the web. He has also blogged for renowned community blogging sites such as SiliconIndia, Instablogs, NowPublic, FoodIndustryIndia, Wayn and SpeakingTree besides his own blogging sites in Blogger and Wordpress in addition to being member of several poetry and writing sites on the internet.

Vincent was one of the directors of the Press Club of India, New Delhi in 2009-10 and nominated member of the 'Legal Committee' of the Press Club of India in 2010-11. He was an adviser to the Delhi Union of Journalists

(2013-14). He is a member of the National Council of the Delhi Union of Journalists for the year 2016-17.

Vincent is a life member of several groups interested in nature and wildlife, writing, photography, art, conservation, environment etc. and has been office bearer on several councils and committees of organizations dealing with social issues, environmental and charitable causes as also promotion and conservation of heritage monuments as well as nature and wildlife.

Unity in Diversity

Indian has twenty-nine states
And, seven union territories
Each state has a different language
And dozens of ethnic groups

There are dozens of religions in India
There are hundreds of dialects
There are thousands of ethnic groups
But, I have an identity of my own

There are all shades of skin in India
From white to sallow
From sallow to brown
And, from brown to dark complexion

Many of us have Caucasian origins
Some look like Mongoloids
Some others have Negroid features
Races of all hues are here

Every state has its culture and costume
Every state has its own cuisine
We are diverse in many different ways
But, we are united as a nation

India is a mini-Asia
India is a mini-World
India is a mini-Universe
It stands for unity in diversity

Indian at Heart

I am an Indian by birth
My name is Vincent Van Ross
People attribute my name
To a Dutch descent

I cannot trace my lineage
To Dutch ancestors
I do not even know
If I have a Dutch connection

I was born and bred in New Delhi
The Capital of India
I have lived all my life here
And, this is the city I love most

I live in the plains
But hills are not far away
We have deserts in the northwest
And, oceans in the south

It is chilly in winter
Sweltering hot in summer
It pours like waterfalls
And, is pleasant during spring

No matter where we come from
No matter where we are settled
No matter what we are
We are Indians at heart

Rava Upma

Rava Upma is a popular south Indian breakfast. It is a simple recipe that is easy to make and fast to cook. Upma is a corrupted form of Uppu Mavu. Uppu means salt and Mavu means flour. Semolina is also a form of wheat flour. Rava means Semolina. Semolina is called Rava in south India and Suji in north India.

Ingredients:

2 Tb spoon oil or clarified butter
1 Tsp Mustard seeds
1 Onion finely chopped
1 Inch ginger grated
1 Green chilli finely chopped
I cup semolina
2 ½ Cups of water
¼ to ½ Tsp Salt or as per taste
2 Tb spoon chopped coriander leaves for garnishing (optional)

Method:

- Heat oil in a pan
- Add: Mustard seeds in hot oil and as it begins to splutter, add onion, ginger and green chilli and sauté for a minute.
- Add: Semolina and sauté till it gets roasted.
- Add: Water and salt and mix well
- Cook for two minutes.
- Rava Upma is ready. If you like, you may garnish it with fresh coriander leaves.

Enjoy this salty dish with accompaniment of your choice. It tastes great even without any accompaniment.

Shades of the Same Skin

Italy

Shades of the Same Skin

Joan Leotta

Ancestry: Italy
Family home: Pennsylvania, USA

Talking about growing up Italian American often results in a discussion about food.

Really when you think about Italy, you probably think at least partly about the food. For those of us who have Italy in our genetic structure, food is a big part of what defines us, has shaped our fondest memories, and makes us stand out to others (especially those who are invited into our homes. Really though, the traditions of food are simply an outgrowth of other aspects of Italian culture. Food is the vehicle by which we carry that culture into modern American life, into future generations and our family histories but what powers that engine is a strong love of family.

I grew up in Pittsburgh, a few miles from my cousins, Aunts, Uncles and my beloved Grandmother. Sundays we all gathered at her house. My best friends were my cousins. My closest confidante was my Grandmother. Moreover, often our "secrets" were shared while she prepared food for an upcoming family dinner or holiday celebration.

Food is central to my concept of my identity as an Italian –American. First, Italian food's basic concept is that it must be the best available product on the market, prepared simply and served to everyone at table, thus, the tradition of Sunday suppers with the extended family and mealtime together, nightly if possible with the nuclear family.

My husband and I both had pasta at least twice weekly growing up. We continued that tradition when we had children, but what made us really and out culturally was the enforcement of daily supper with the four of us, every night. We gritted our teeth and changed mealtimes often to satisfy the demands of the local soccer league for practices that bulldozed across our regular meal hour. We endued whining—"No one else has to eat with their family" when teens wanted to leave early for a party We reaped the benefit when our daughter started to preach this philosophy among her friends and told us that others envied our family and loved coming to our house where everyone ate dinner together.

Holidays and Sundays - as adults, we lived too far from extended family to have a Sunday with everyone (several hundred miles). However, the four of us carried on the seven fishes and opening of gifts on Christmas Eve and my husband and I told tales of our own childhoods when grandparents, aunts, uncles and cousins also joined in. We reinforced that by spending part of our children's school holiday on the road to actually celebrate the holiday with family on both sides (three days each) even if was not on the actual night of Christmas Eve.

We invite people into our home and stay at the table with conversation. Everyone who can speak is welcome to join in. All opinions are welcome. We like to talk. We like to listen.

Therefore, in that regard, I am sharing a short story, a poem and photos along the theme of food and family gatherings.

Christmas Eve at my grandmother's house. My father, my grandmother (my mother's mother) and I (around age five).

Shades of the Same Skin

The Oak Table Discussion

This small story is a tale of how our dinners set us apart from even other adults. My cousin's friend (we will call her Rhoda here) was coming to our city. My cousin called me.

"Joan can you invite my friend Rhoda to dinner at your house next week? She is considering moving to your area for a job and does not know anyone."

Of course, my answer was a resounding yes. I took the woman's name down and called her. She was very happy to accept for a Wednesday night dinner, which dovetailed nicely with an appointment with potential employers—not far from our suburban home.

Knowing she would probably expect an Italian meal, I prepared roasted chicken with rosemary, a side dish of rigatoni in a sauce with eggplant and green peppers, a lovely salad and fruit and ice cream for dessert. This menu was also one of my husband's favorites. Our children were mostly neutral although our son hated eggplant and our daughter moaned every time I served rigatoni, so I made a plain sauce side of fusilli for them—with enough to serve our guest in case her taste buds were more inclined to vote with those of our children.

She arrived just before the meal. My husband had been home for twenty minutes. The children had picked flowers for the table. All was well. Because it was a school night and the children would be leaving the table to go into the den to do homework and eat their dessert with a side of math problems, we ate in the eat-in kitchen rather than the formal dining room.
Our guest did not seem to mind sitting at table quickly.

Rhoda was a very intelligent and accomplished woman. My husband and I asked her about her interviews and she revealed an interest in some of the major political issues of the day. When she had just finished expounding on some aspect of that issue, our ten-year-old daughter, Jennie asked a question that sliced across Rhoda's logical presumptions. Rhoda looked amazed. She stumbled over a few words to try to defend her position.
Then our eight-year-old son, called that answer into question based on logic and consistency with Rhoda's earlier statements. Rhoda's reply was calm but her eyes blazed. She turned to me with a look of "Really?" I noted her visibly recoil when I guess she noticed that I was beaming! I was so proud of my

children. They were following the discussion. They were participating. We were not talking Ninja turtles! This was for real—just as when I grew up. My husband was beaming in the same way. We were cultivating a pair of people who had opinions and knew how to express them. Their questions were offered in a respectful tone of voice; however, our guest was appalled. She left so soon after desert that I think the coffee in her cup was still warm when I removed it from the table to the sink.

I later learned that she told my cousin that she had never heard of anyone allowing children to talk at the table like that.to question an adult. My reaction - "What planet is she from?"

My more Americanized (on this issue) cousin laughed in reply, "Not everyone considers it fair game to speak your mind at the dinner table as soon as you can speak!"

In fact, she also told me that some people in our generation not only no longer ate together on weeknights, but also had the children eat separately when they had adult guests, as a regular pattern, not on the occasional dinner party.

Now I was the one reeling and the one who realized that indeed we were unusual and had preserved the Italian side in our hyphenated identities—Italian-American.

On the Making of *Pizzelle*

"Please write your recipe for *pizzelle*,"
Mama answered, "Words are not enough."
That very afternoon, together,
we measured, stirred,
matching the day's humidity
with the correct amount of flour.
She let me stir too
so I could feel, "just right."
We oiled her special press.
Two hours later we
proudly out set a plate of
light, barely browned, pizzelle,
crisp with hints of vanilla and anise.
Next, she took me to buy a *pizzelle* iron
from the man who sold one to her
and to her mother.

> One of the traditions of holiday time is making *pizzelle*, an Italian cookie shaped like a flat waffle.

Eggplant Parmesan (The way my Grandma made it)

Ingredients:

2 cups marinara sauce
2 small-medium eggplants
Salt
Olive oil
4 eggs
½ cup fresh Flat Italian parsley
½ cup grated *pecorino romano* cheese

Method:

- Slice the eggplant thinly and salt. Allow the slices to stand for at least four hours. Then rinse and press each slice. Either fry the slices in olive oil or brush with oil and bake for fifteen minutes at 350 degrees.
- Beat the eggs with parsley and cheese.
- Preheat oven to 325 degrees.
- Put some sauce on the bottom of a casserole dish. Lay down a layer of eggplant. Pour on some of the egg mix, some sauce, repeat until all ingredients are used up. Pour some sauce on top.
- Bake for 45 minutes to one hour.

Shades of the Same Skin

England

Laura Marie Clark

From and currently resides: England, UK.

I was born and raised in a tiny village. No church, no shop, no village hall … the isolation developed two opposite aspects of my personality: my nervous, shy love of being alone, and my wish to live somewhere vibrant, active and loud.

As a teenager, I went on a Polish exchange trip with school, which was the first time I had really – though temporarily – felt immersed in another culture. That was when I realised how much there is out there to discover, both at home and abroad.

Later, when I lived in Vietnam, I felt a huge change in the way that I wrote, and spent more of my time writing poetry and focusing on (usually negative) emotions and human experiences. I had seen how some of the poorer people there lived and I wanted to share this through my writing.

For this anthology, I've decided to show the lighter side of my writing. I think that culture should be fun so that it can encourage people who haven't heard those stories or seen those objects before to learn more about them.

The poem I've provided, The Lincoln Imp, is a common folk talk about the statue of an imp that is carved into the stonework of Lincoln cathedral. The short story Almost an Egyptian Bride is a true story from my early teenage years, during a family holiday in Luxor. The photograph provides me with precious memories from Vietnam.

To me, these are not separate parts of my life. Each cultural story has helped to build me into the person I am today. I am not English or British. I am a combination of everything I have experienced so far in my life.

Laura's page: www.ctupublishinggroup.com/laura-marie-clark.html

Almost an Egyptian Bride

I am worth half a herd of camels.

"That's an odd thing to say," I hear you respond. "How would you know that?"

On a family holiday in Egypt, we rode camels along the Nile, in a group of tourists. Each camel was led by an Egyptian. We talked to them, the sort of idle chatter that tourists like to make.

As I remember it, the guy who was leading my camel was a bit older than me – I was only in my early teenage years at the time. We had been flirting a little, the kind of innocent flirting that shy teenagers exchange on a first date. It was cute and harmless.

My parents, close by, also began chatting to this young man after a while. My dad has always liked to laugh at my holiday romances – and my boyfriends at home. He has this calm, casual manner that makes those awkward first encounters feel easier. At least for me, anyway.

They joked around for a while. At some point in the conversation, the guy who was leading my camel made what I thought was a strange offer: half of his herd of twenty camels, in exchange for which I would become his bride.

One of the things I love so much about my parents is that they can handle this sort of situation so well. They ummed and they erred, and they speculated over what they would do with ten camels when they got them home. That was when they hit the snag in the plan.

How were they supposed to get ten camels back to the UK in a small suitcase?

And so I returned home with my family, camel-less, but proud in the new knowledge that I was worth half a herd of camels, which seems pretty good to me.

The Lincoln Imp

They say that the imp, a mischievous fellow
Was sent by the Devil in evil to revel

In league with his brother, he smashed tables and chairs,
Then the bishop they tripped – and over he flipped!

These naughty creatures, they say, were surprised
When a prayer book nearby announced with a cry

The arrival of an angel who told them: "Now, cease,
Go back from where you came" – to one imp, in vain

Bravely this imp stood against Heaven's sent,
At the angel cast rocks; great power he mocked

While his friend, a coward, fled from the sight
Hid under the rubble they'd caused in their trouble

The angel, in his might, turned the first imp to stone
And he sits to this day in the cathedral, they say

To the second, the angel: "Now, I give you this chance
To escape what I was sent to deliver: your punishment."

And they say the second imp still circles the cathedral
Searching without end for his cold, grey, stone friend

Cultural Photo

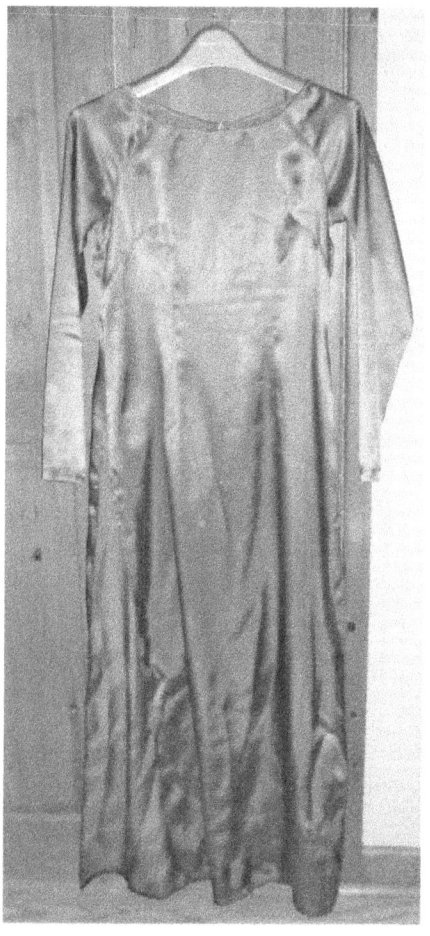

This is an example of traditional Vietnamese clothing, called áo dài. It is a silk tunic and it is worn over trousers. The style has been updated many times, but the modern style was designed in the 1950s. It is used for formal occasions, such as weddings, Tét (Vietnamese New Year), school and graduation. The dress is supposed to link beauty to nationalism.

Lynn White

From and currently resides: England, UK

I live in a rural, one time industrial area in the mountains of north Wales. I was born in industrial Sheffield. Both my parents families migrated there from country areas to find work in the steel industry.

My work is influenced by my surroundings, past and present, and the effect of the demise of industry has on the landscape and the people inhabiting it. Some change over time - issues of social justice and events, places and people I have known or imagined feature in my work.

I am especially interested in exploring the boundaries of dream, fantasy and reality.

Lynn's pages:

www.facebook.com/Lynn-White-Poetry-1603675983213077/

lynnwhitepoetry.blogspot.com

Ripples

Ripples of time
gathering pace.
Working up to the wave
that crashed into me,
propelled me forward
and now sucks me back.
Thirteen decades.
Back.
To a place beyond my imagining,
so tidy now after the crash.
Gentrified now.
Rippling gently.
But before,
in my father's time.
There was beer mixed mud
and crowding children.
And smells of horses
and metal.
Working.
Fire and metal work.
Children who
would leave behind
the mud,
and country
smells,
for the dust
and smog.
For the city grime.
Streets and factories.
More fire and metal.
Bigger.
Grander.
And what then?
Still poor.
What then?
What secrets lie in those ripples
of time washing over me
now.

A Grey Place?

This is a grey place,
there's no denying.
Grey slate, grey granite,
grey houses built of both.
And it rains a lot, there's no denying.
Vertical, or horizontal, or swirling rain
falling greyly from heavy misty clouds.
But when caught by a sunbeam
it makes glistening slides
shimmering across the slate
and falls in bright white tails
or snakes like silver
where the mountains leak it.
And spills heavily over rocks,
it's foaming, frothing, yellow ruffed
cascades catching rainbows as they crash
then spitting them back out
in a fine spray of colours.
And now there's no grey
in the dark blue, black sky
filled with gold and silver twinkles.
No grey at all in this place now,
there's no denying.

Shades of the Same Skin

Caribbean Islands

Shades of the Same Skin

Puerto Rico

Shades of the Same Skin

Shirley Ann Cooper

From: Puerto Rico
Currently resides: Florida, USA

Coming from a multicultural family, I have learned to examine the world from the inside out. Because of my cultural background, my eyes are opened to new things, whether through the fashion industry or the food world. I enjoy the many colors that pour out into my life and the culture that follows.

My life has been a tremendous teacher, leading me to an amazing journey that breathes life into my soul. I thank my God that I am able to understand others more every day and the lives they live, through their cultural background.

Being mixed of two nationalities, Puerto Rican and Filipino, has helped me in the way I express myself through my writing. I am able to grasp the reality that every blood is different; A beautiful rainbow of colors. The wide spread phenomenon in the foodie department has been quite fascinating, and it's a blessing to know that the food I was raised enjoying has shaken the culinary world.

I was born in Ceiba, Puerto Rico, with my mother being Puerto Rican and my father being Filipino. Although I have never stepped foot into the Philippines, I learned how to cook the food well. It's been a long time since I've had the pleasure of indulging in the beautiful island I was born on, but hope to one day return.

Today, I reside in McAlpin, Florida with my husband of 32 years. I am the mother of four amazing children, with wonderful in-laws that I love very much. I'm a grandmother to the cutest grand kids, who all now share and enjoy the culture I was so blessed to soak in.

Shades of the Same Skin

No matter where I stand, I will always take pride in the blood that runs freely through my veins.

Shirley's page:

https://m.facebook.com/From-Heaven-ablog- 219583824881505/

My Island, Beautiful

My Island, beautiful. It's where I was blessed enough to live my first five years of life. The beautiful beaches and the smell of the ocean were just captivating.

I remember playing in the sand and running from the land crabs and huge bullfrogs. On my island, these crustaceans and amphibians are famous, especially a tiny frog the size of a pinky nail, called the Coqui. They are celebrities found in books, television and bedtime stories. These faint memories certainly bring back the little girl who once spoke in her native language. It brings tears to my eyes as the island carries more than my youth. It's a place where my parents fell in love.

The sun in Puerto Rico is absolutely gorgeous, along with the palm trees, and the coconuts that clung to them. Let's not forget the food. How delicious a life? I thank God that today I am able to share my life on the island with my children, through cooking.

The many foods cooked from the homes of the island people blended well with the tropical breeze, making every taste bud close by fill up with saliva. I remember being at my aunt's house for dinner and the main course – pork - was celebrated. I had no idea what that meant until the food was done and everyone went outside to eat. Mom made pork all the time, so no big deal, right?

Wrong! When I looked out into the field, what I discovered would change the way I welcomed food. There in front of me was a large pig on a pole, above a fire. I ran away faster than I did when I was being chased by land crabs.

I must say, that I truly miss my Island, beautiful, and hope to one day return.

El Yunque Intertwined With My Heart

The smell of rain filled my nostrils like an overwhelming joy,
The breeze that followed every step would drown out all the noise.
Each time I walked or ran through the forest grounds,
I'd find myself lost in the beauty of the sound.
The beautiful chirps of tropical feathered friends,
Would stay embedded in my ears to never end.
The waterfalls that stretched far and wide,
Would be my partner and my guide.
The scenery and wildlife that stood still adorned my eyes,
As it captivated my heart and became mine.
In search of peace I discovered something new,
The peaceful life of the Caribbean shined through.
The concession stand that smelled of delicious island delicacies,
Made taste buds wild and tickled the belly.
The stars shined brighter than the sun itself,
The dark skies made every heart just melt.
My feet felt the stones that lay still,
As I walked over every bump and hill.
I remember when the time drew near,
To leave this place made me tear.
The dance poured out as the end came close,
This is the place I'll miss the most.
When memories are shared they'll never spark,
Like that gorgeous place that grabbed my heart.
El Yunque, the rain forest dream,
Became everything it intended to be.
As the distance kept us far apart,
It will forever be intertwined with my heart.

Red & Pink Beans

No matter where or when you get the chance to finally make this recipe, I hope that you, your loved ones, and friends, enjoy my homes most beloved meal.

SERVINGS - 8 UNITS (US)

INGREDIENTS:

- 1 (16 ounce) can red kidney beans (habichuelas coloradas) and 1 (16 ounce) can pink beans (habichuelas coloradas)
- 1 teaspoon adobo seasoning (a flavored salt used in Latin cooking)
- 4 tablespoon vegetable oil
- 1/2 stick butter or margarine
- 1 - 1/2 cup large cubed boneless rib pork meat with fat
- 2 teaspoons garlic cloves (chopped)
- 1 teaspoon garlic powder
- 1/2 teaspoon black pepper
- 3 (5g) packet sazon with azafran seasoning (comes in envelopes in a box, gives color and a distinct flavor to latin dishes)
- 3 tablespoons Sofrito sauce and 3 tablespoons Recaito sauce (comes in a jar, a necessary ingredient in Puerto Rican cuisine)

Note: you can make these sauces homemade as well to give this dish an even more authentic taste.

- 1 can of Goya tomato sauce

DIRECTIONS:

- In saucepan, heat oil on low-medium heat and put in the pork.
- Once it starts to sizzle, add the garlic powder, and chopped garlic cloves, black pepper and Adobo seasoning.
- Then add the Sofrito and Sazon con Azafran seasoning, stir.
- Slowly stir in tomato sauce.
- Next add red beans, add butter.
- Cook to a boil. Mix well. Cover with lid and simmer.
- Serve with Goya short grain white rice. (Spanish style)

Shades of the Same Skin

(On my island beautiful, Puerto Rico, it's traditional to serve rice and beans with almost every meal, with Spanish style pork chops and fried garlic plantains on the side) The rice must be Spanish style as well. Using Crisco lard and salt during the cooking process.

Shades of the Same Skin

Jamaica

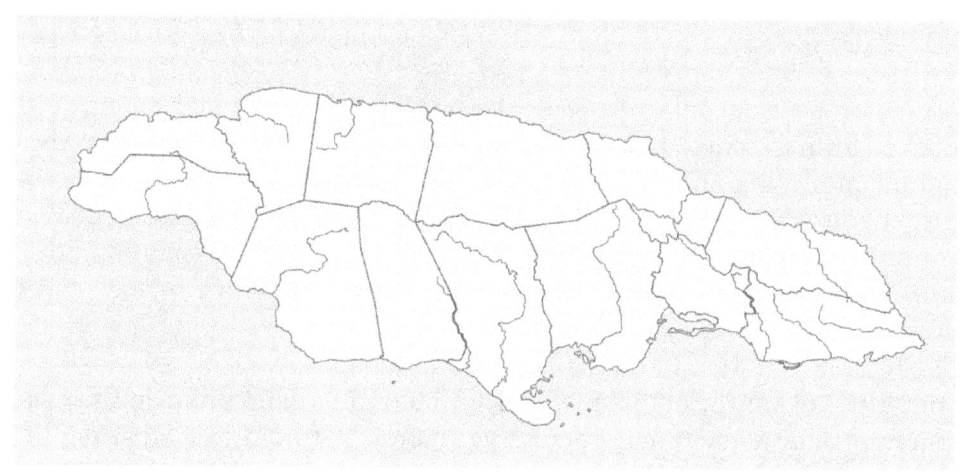

Christena AV Williams

From and currently resides: Jamaica

Poet and Author of *Pearls among Stones.*

I am from Portmore, otherwise known as "sunshine City." The place I am from is everything you can experience. It is a unique place indeed from the mountains, food, music, people, dance, language, sports, politics, nature's paradise everything culture.

I am what is consider mix breed, as the history of slavery and colonization have given birth to people like me. While these are bitter times in history, there is slight appreciation and this has shaped the person I am today couple with life experiences as a child of father abandoned and poverty-stricken. "Whey mi come from" This is called patois or Creole I am from the melting pot of cultures where sun kisses the beaches magnificently and while music soothes your soul.

We run fast and we rock rhythms, and we culturally expressive and yes, not ashamed to share violent and aggressive, but do not hold it against us. It is deep rooted warrior spirit that fought our oppressors brewing inside of us, as many are from the Ashanti tribe. We are Africans in The Americas.

This will that we have to fight can be seen on the tracks, which amazes the world, and our ability to survive harsh conditions in a country that is economically depleted by poor management and exploitation of our past oppressors. This will you see, displayed in our music and sports are in our DNA, and are unexplainable to some but a lot is to do with our history. I could go on and on about this place and give you everything great and bad but I am from "welcome to Jam rock by Junior Gong Marley would sang it" Jamaica.

Christena's page: http://amzn.com/1507600453

Shades of the Same Skin

Out of Many, One People

Beat the Congo
Blow the horn
Wave your hand
Out of many one people
What a vibration
In a this little island

Even though we cannot live as one
But when a party time
We unite
Nuh matter the culture (it does not)
We a full joy we self
You have Rasta talking
Christians praying
Bay song playing (in the context Bay means a lot)
Smiles on everybody faces
Out of many one people

So come the Chinese, British, Syrians, Americans, Indians
Every Caribbean and rest of the world
Come to Jamaica
And feel alright
Listen some Bob
Do not carry any jewelry
Because you will get rob
But come and eat
Have a feast
Enjoy we beach
Entertainment

Energy a shot
Dink a cold beer
Relax under the coconut tree
Feel free
We have jerk chicken
Curry goat
Festival, rice, Bammy
Fry and steam fish

Shades of the Same Skin

Come enjoy we cultural dish
Food galore
Go back a your country
Tell every boy and girl
Say Jamaica nice

We know say crime and violence
Corruption
A plague
But don't let that stop you
Cause everybody welcome
Nuh matter taste (It doesn't)
Come in a haste
Cause we have a celebration
Jam dung vibration
Me a tell the politician
Say me a send out a special invitation
But first we yard need renovation
Build up Jamaica
And education
Cause we live in a paradise
Black, green and gold
We proud and bold
As we motto say
Out of many, one people.

Shades of the Same Skin

The Great Reggae Legend

Born Robert Nesta Marley on February 6, 1945
In nine mile, St.Ann
Emancipate yourself from mental slavery none
Ourselves can free our mind
I grew up on that prophetic message and philosophy
It never left my soul or mind
You have left a legacy
World-renowned
This dreadlocks man left his mark
Permanently

I believe you were before your time
I was not yet born
When you departure
As your music was my friend
I was built on your roots
Something music lacks today
Your words emanate so powerfully
That builds faith and tear down injustice
It inspire greatness

I remember the man who chants words of ball of fire
Hitting beyond anyone's imagination
Or comprehension of his God given talent
He has touched hearts from Jamaica to America
Europe to India to Africa all over
His music is worldwide
It is like a life's guide
Whether ball head or Rasta man
Bob Marley music lives on
I have yet to see someone like him
His legacy continues with his sons and daughters
With every Jamaican
His message was deep, spiritual and philosophical
To the soul and mind.

R.I.P
The Great Reggae Legend.

Shades of the Same Skin

Jamaican Recipe for Mango Smoothie

Ingredients:

- 2 ripe mangos
- 2 oranges
- 2 cups yogurt (plain or flavored – vanilla or orange are both good)
- 2 teaspoons honey
- ¼ cup dark rum (optional)
- 10 ice cubes
- A dash of ground nutmeg
- A dash of ground cinnamon.

Directions:

1. Peel the mango and dice into ice cube sized chunks. Place in a plastic bag and freeze for an hour.

2. Remove the mango chunks from the freezer and place in a blender container.

3. Add yogurt, honey, ice cubes and rum (if you are using it).

4. Juice the oranges (with a juicer or by squeezing) and pour juice and pulp into the blender.

5. Blend on high for about 1 minute or until smooth. Add the nutmeg and cinnamon on top. Stir.

6. Divide into glasses and garnish with spears of mango or thin slices of orange. SERVES 2-3

Recipe Credit: Winsome Murphy

Shades of the Same Skin

Trinidad & Tobago

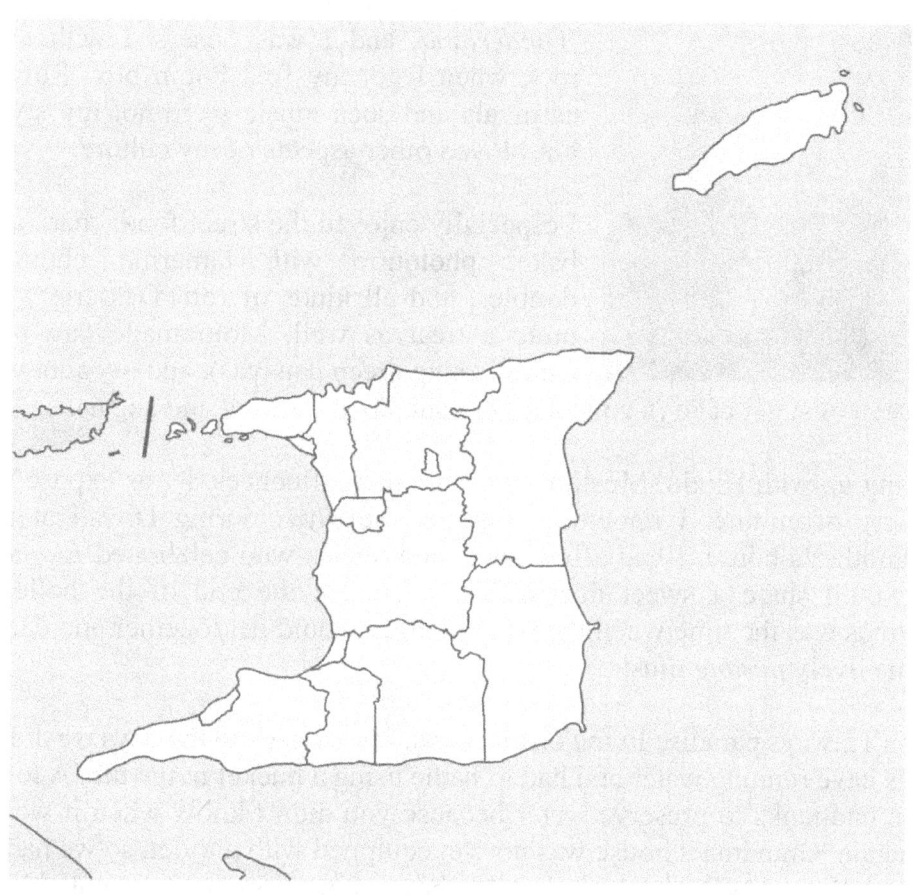

Donna J. Sanders

From: Trinidad
Currently resides: Florida, USA

I wasn't quite the typical island girl. I buried my head in Nancy Drew books, I wore out the record player listening to a narrative of *Alice in Wonderland*, and I was obsessed with 80's rock when I got my first boom box. Rowdy carnivals and soca music were not my style, but I loved other aspects of my culture.

I especially enjoyed the street food: shark and bake, pholourie with tamarind chutney, doubles, and all kinds of roti. Desserts were quite a treat as well. Mom made paw-paw candy (using green papayas), and my aunt was the queen of sugar cake (a concoction of shredded coconut and sugar).

Growing up with Hindu, Muslim, and Christian influences, I was exposed to a variety of culture. I remember lighting the *diyas* during Diwali at my grandmother's house. I had a few aunts and uncles who celebrated *Eid*, and they would share a sweet dish called *sawine* at the end of the holiday. Christmas was the time when the whole family would get together and dance to some lively *parang* music.

It wasn't always paradise living on an island. I think back to the days we didn't always have running water and had to bathe using a bucket in the tub. A lot of people had tanks to preserve water because you didn't know when it would flow again. Grandma's house was not yet equipped with a toilet, so we had to use the latrine outside. I remain humble because my parents were not able to afford everything I wanted, which is why today, I am not obsessed with having the latest items trending or brand named goods.

Everything I experienced on the island has certainly influenced my writing and my way of life. I hope as I continue to write, I can inform and entertain using the culture flowing through my veins.

> ***Diyas*** – oil lamp made from clay used in religious festivals or ceremonies
>
> ***Eid*** – a religious holiday celebrated by Muslims
>
> ***Sawine*** – a sweet dish to celebrate the end of fasting, make with milk, vermicelli noodles and flavored with aromatic spices.
>
> ***Parang*** – folk music brought to Trinidad by Venezuelan migrants, with Spanish and African influences.

Donna's pages:

www.facebook.com/DonnaJSanders6825

https://theraven6825.wordpress.com/

www.ctupublishinggroup.com/donna-j.-sanders.html

Shades of the Same Skin

Pelau

She would yell,
Beti, go pick some pigeon peas for meh.

I would run to the backyard where she had
peas and scotch bonnet pepper trees

I loved eating the pods right out of the shells

Watching her catch a chicken was entertainment
They were fast on their three pronged feet
but not fast enough for grandma's machete

The fowl had no time to feel pain

Immediately soaking it in boiling water
I helped her pluck the feathers from its warm skin
and then she chopped it to pieces

The fresh meat would marinate in her green seasoning
with some salt and chunks of pepper

She would stand at the stove in her flamingo stance
stirring the huge iron pot stained with years of curry

Nobody could make a pelau like grandma could

Beti (bay – tee) – means daughter in Hindi, could also be used as dear/darling

Pelau – chicken is seared in caramelized brown sugar - rice and peas are added then simmered in coconut milk. Not an easy dish to make. I've tried it once and failed. I leave this one to the professionals.

Shades of the Same Skin

Cultural Photo

The iron pot is a must have in every Caribbean household. It can be made of cast iron or aluminum, but the cast iron ones are much better for cooking curries and stews that need to simmer low and slow. These pots last such a long time; they can be passed down from generation to generation.

Trinidad Green Seasoning

Ingredients:

- 1 medium onion (peeled and chopped)
- 4 scallions (aka green onions - chopped)
- 1 celery stalk (chopped)
- 10-12 cloves garlic (peeled)
- 4-5 sprigs fresh thyme (chopped with stems removed)
- 1 bunch fresh cilantro or culantro (chopped)
- water

Optional ingredients:

scotch bonnet or habanero pepper
red pepper flakes
hot sauce
parsley
green pepper
red pepper

Directions:

- Place all ingredients in food processor or blender, adding water a little at a time until desired consistency. Texture should be like pesto.

  Use on any type of meat to marinate overnight.

You can also just finely chop everything instead of blending

Can also use olive oil instead of water but since olive oil can tenderize meat, shorten the time for seafood and leaner cuts of beef.

This seasoning is best when used fresh, but you can make a large batch and freeze in portions for future use. Fresh can be stored for about 1 week in refrigerator.

Shades of the Same Skin

USA

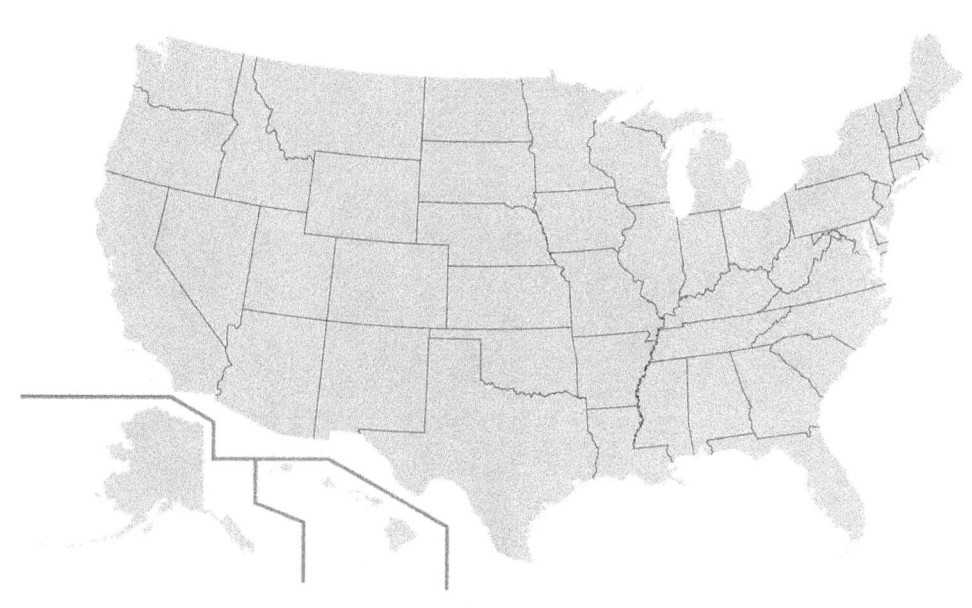

Shades of the Same Skin

Michigan

Ryan Vallee

From and currently resides: Michigan, USA

Michigan, born and raised. If I lifted an outstretched hand to you, and pointed to the thumb, that's exactly where. 4 miles from the beach of Lake Huron. 4 miles from farmlands.

You can run from the Motor City, the steel presses and hot sparks of industry, to the calloused hands of farmers digging at the fields. You can climb Sleeping Bear Dunes to scoop sand that rivals that of any Florida beach. You can walk north through Mackinac, and stand in the humid heat of the fudge shops, watching as they flip and flop chocolate layers on big slabs of marble before sampling it fresh. Cross the bridge to the upper peninsula, travel highways cut through unpolished lands, heavy forest, to find places with names such as Paradise, and the Lake of the Clouds.

It really is paradise at times, in a "crazy ex" kind of way. I've worn flip-flops and snow boots in the same week. I've built sandcastles and snowmen just days apart. I've walked the beach on Christmas Eve and ran the furnace on the Fourth of July. I kind of like it though. It's built character in us here.

We are hardworking folks. Blue collar. We've been brought up with edge and merit. We accept the cold just the same as we embrace the warmth. Our soul doesn't just swim on the skin, it's as deep as the Great Lakes themselves.

Ryan's pages:

www.instagram.com/ryan.vallee

www.ctupublishinggroup.com/ryan-vallee.html

Shades of the Same Skin

The Boy Who Buried His Dog in the Sand

There was a boy that buried his dog in the sand.
he was just playing.
it was incredibly warm in the sun, one of those
afternoons where it seemed even the air was crying out.
his mom told him so.
"you're going to lose him burying him like that" she said.
there was no other way though, you see, the enemy troops
were advancing quick and the dog was just showing our
good guys where to hide. he barked a few warnings, burrowed
into the sand (down deep where it was still cool) and that was
the last he was seen.
in life we call this a casualty of war.
tell this to the boy digging frantically.
mom says I told you so.
but as a good mother does, she's digging just the same.

the boy doesn't cry over much anymore, but he does over this.

each time they return to the beach, he paces out the rough area
like a foreman ready to break ground, and digs.

less and less, of course.
time has had its lessons, and it has healed almost as well.
he still wonders after the dog, and what became of him.

is he still under the sand somewhere, lying in his gritty grave?

did the tide finally reach high enough to pull him free, finding
wave after wave, cold under every sunset?

did some other boy, near his age, happen to dig him up like a buried
treasure, or stub his toe on him, picking him up and playing on in some
new battle, some new imagination?

he likes to imagine it the latter, like some strange reincarnation.
and thinks that would be nice for us all.

Shades of the Same Skin

Cultural Photo

This picture is my 3 kids Fayth, Ava and Ivan, at the tip of the thumb of Michigan.

Some days the lake looks like the ocean up there. Here you can watch both the sunrise and the sunset over the water.

Shades of the Same Skin

New York

Nolan P. Holloway

From: New York, USA
Currently Resides: Georgia, USA

Both my parents were from the South but my brother, sister and I were raised in Queens, NY. In a neighborhood of black people who were proud homeowners.

Every summer we drove to visit both my parents' hometowns. My father was from Jacksonville, Florida and my mother from Aliceville, Alabama. My dad graduated from Tuskegee, served in the Navy, met and married my mom and moved up North for a better opportunity.

Proud to call New York the place of my birth; Atlanta is now my home. And this is the place where my gift to write poetry took flight.

Nolan's pages:

www.nolanphollowayjr.com

www.ctupublishinggroup.com/nolan-p.-holloway--jr..html

Outer Layer

Skin is just a coloring
A reflection of God's image
But racial tensions keep bubbling
Generation to generation we hope
That we can live together in peace
Mindsets of hate make it difficult to cope
I am proud of my skin
Shade of caramel, smooth candy brown
Feelings of where my ancestors have been
Dreams of bonding to each other in love
Practicing the agape way of Jesus
Staying true to what is above
Knowing that when our spirits are transformed
All the shades will be reborn

Face of the Mandrill

A myriad of colors vibrantly blended
What a lovely thought if people could embrace without being external
Following differences needing understanding
Opening to Love in all directions
Waiting for the feelings to boomerang
Hands raised in reverence
Not to surrender but freedom of submission
Gaining from the loss of hate
Being a slave to truth
Outer continence to reveal what the true nature of the internal could be
Gazing upon the image created in the likeness of the Father of All

Cultural Photo

My father and mother.

Shades of the Same Skin

North Carolina

David Hall

From and currently resides: North Carolina, USA

David Hall was born in a small town called Mount Airy (A.K.A Mayberry) nestled in the foothills of the Blue Ridge Mountains which are part of the large Appalachian Mountain chain.

His early life involved a lot of traveling with his missionary parents, which involved stints of living in Mexico and Bolivia. His poetry reflects a love for nature and life mixed with a sense of the rustic Americana spirit and sprinkled with a lingering sense of the spiritual guidance infused by his southern religious upbringing.

David has always been able to live in the moment enjoying it to the fullest while being able to be separated within himself seeking something more.

Poetry is one of those outlets that gives him that something more. The diversity of genres and endless array of topics allow him to dive into poetry with reckless abandon or with fine-tuned precision; whichever is needed. Like a prism there are many sides of David, from the emotional connections when dealing with death, to the touch of the spring breeze on your neck hairs, David's poetry can put you there.

David's page: www.ctupublishinggroup.com/d.b.-hall.html

The Bent Tree

When I was a boy running wild through the Appalachian backwoods with my buddies, we came across an odd shaped tree. It was a bent tree; one of those old Indian bent trees that we'd heard about in the old stories. We let our imagination go wild. We climbed it, jumped off it, rode it like the Lone Ranger on Silver, and pretended we were Blackbeard sailing on Queen Anne's Revenge; marauding up and down the coast of the Carolinas. Indiana Jones had nothing on us in our harrowing escapades. We were happy kids enjoying our carefree summer under our favorite hangout. Within our little group, we made a solemn pact to tell no one about our secret spot.

One day my parents told me the rather disturbing news that our family would be moving as missionaries to another country. A country in South America called Bolivia. I was pretty tore up about it, unsure about that foreign place. We made the best of the rest of the summer but as the days come closer to the day my family had to go, a difference began to fall upon us. At our young ages, goodbye was something we had never experienced and so it meant forever. My buddies and I were pretty distraught during that last week and in an important pact of friendship, we decided to put a few treasured items in a box and bury it under our tree and then open it when I came back from the trip. It was not much; some prized rookie baseball cards, a few favorite Hot Wheels, we also each put in one rusted knife. Mine was a rusted but awesome Barlow that had this nick in the blade out toward the end. I had rescued it from the mud on the side of the road. I had sharpened it as best I could but that was a bad nick and I just couldn't get it out. All in all not very fancy stuff, but very special to us because somehow we knew our friendship was special and this tree was too, though we didn't know why.

Years later, finally back home in familiar country with stomachs full of grandma's good ol home cookin, only two of us made that journey back through those woods. So many things had changed, trees were bigger and paths were now overgrown. Some friendships were not as strong as they once were but our tree was still there, the sapling sprouts were tall trees kissing the sky. We no longer fit under our tree near as easy as we did before. Corny as it may seem to some but to us it was very exciting. We grinned like fools and started digging after a bit of arguing over where to start at and several shoulder punches. We dug at one spot and then another and then dug some more, but finally had to admit our treasure box was gone. We accepted the fact that greed had struck one of our old buddies. We weren't really mad. Kinda hated

Shades of the Same Skin

it, but the comradery and experience were what it was about. We ended up sitting back against the tree laughing, two cousins who were truly brothers for life, and so life would prove we were, though short that would turn out to be.

Years later, I found myself on a Kubota tractor working the devil out of a front end loader near that old hangout behind grandma's. A little after midday, I was wiping a ton of sweat off my face, reminiscing quite a bit and becoming quite teary-eyed. As I traveled through the woods they became a bit sparser and I was seriously lamenting the fact that the harshness of life dictated that I had to travel through them alone. Still yet, I could not resist traveling back to that ol place. Our beautiful tree was gone, chopped down before their time, just like my cousin. I stood back from the edge of the woods and watched a ray of sun touch the young sprouts jumping on the trampoline. Smiling, I knew I was not watching them alone.

Of the Past and Now

Nestled in these gorgeous Carolina foothills
Far away from the bright lights of big city thrills
A panoramic valley blessed with scenic rivers
Fertile lands like their people proven to be givers

These people mostly humble, in worn out overalls
Plowing their fields with patched up Farmalls
Longtime friends visiting on the front porch
Good will is a multi-generational torch

Kids helping grandparents string beans for hours
Grown ripe to perfection from spring showers
Now all those ol dirt roads have been paved
My Mayberry is embracing the new waves

For now comes upon us a different time
Our fields of harvest yield grapes for wine
A tobacco barn is now a rustic antique store
Tourists can now take a scenic winery tour

Websites with linked maps showing the way
Committees with plans for bright new days
Interlinked walking paths and biking trails
Spoken Word Society and Storytelling tails

We still love our country roots and sounds
They are firmly planted deep in these grounds
Autumn Leaves Festivals and Mayberry Days
Are here to remind us about the good ol ways

Looking to the future and making plans
For time marches on, it stops for no man

Rusty Shuping

From and currently resides: North Carolina, USA

Rusty lives in the Southeastern area of USA. This slice of paradise runs through North Carolina and is commonly called the Bible Belt due to its long held tradition and culture stemming from the strong presence of Christianity.

He began to take writing seriously later in life when he learned that experience and life lessons could provide useful content for creative writing. Much of this was brought about through the instruction of Melissa Kepley and Ginger Fox, college instructors of classes attended by Shuping.

Travel has provided mental material, along with the love for growing food and flowers. Recording events in the form of art through photography has also had a huge part in the creative development, which leads into writing. Working with metal for years also worked its role in influencing life decisions. Handling materials with anything from jeweler's tweezers to drilling derricks contributed to a sense of depth in using words to bring life to cerebral commotion.

Rusty writes mostly for self-satisfaction but when words can be used to encourage others it is a big plus. One example is creating real paper, custom greeting cards, and mailing them all over the world.

Morning Word

Yesterday started as an unusually beautiful sunny Sunday. I was standing in the church auditorium. It was getting close to time for the second service to start and I noticed Jim coming through the double doors into the sanctuary. Jim, tall and very thin was dressed warmly with his thick, long sleeved shirt, and a brown toboggan covering his head. He was moving slowly with the aid of his walker. Cancer had emaciated his body. He knew he didn't have long left in this world. I turned and looked toward John who was two rows back from me. I said. "No one has an excuse for not being in church this morning." He smiled and agreed.

Jim and I greeted each other and he sat behind me that morning. He tried to stand when the rest of us but his strength wouldn't allow it for long. His strength gave out and John caught him helping him rest softly into his chair, and Jim settled in for the remainder of a wonderful church service. The singing and preaching were soon over, and Jim wobbled to his feet.

That afternoon I heard that Jim, at 2:00, was sitting in his recliner chair resting. Jim slipped out of his beat up, broken down body, and he went home to be with Jesus in Heaven. Thoughts began running through my mind. Here was a man I was talking to one minute, and not much more than an hour later is in the presence of God for eternity. What a glorious way to start one day, with the sun shining on ones face, and finish it in the presence of the Son of God and to see His face. If we truly know Christ as our Savior we are already living in eternity. We only change locations when it's time to go.

The Shop

Across the drive was the shop. Now the shop was the greatest place in the world for a boy in the country, well any normal boy for that matter. It was filled with antique tools and equipment. Fifty-some years ago they were antique, now even more so. There were so many things for a boy to ask questions about.

Grandpa was very patient and I believe he enjoyed spending time with me, describing all of the neat stuff and showing me how it worked to the point of letting me try most of it. I could write a book on the stuff in that shop. One of my favorite things was the blacksmith forge and the anvil. The buffalo forge had a hand crank and would send a stream of air with a whirring noise into the firebox. Burning coal had a distinctive odor, especially the cheap kind, with all of the Sulphur. It would burn your eyes and give you a runny nose until it was burning good. Then it would heat up the steel tools very quickly.

I liked watching Grandpa sharpen cold chisels, mattocks, and other small implements. The heating and hammering, over and over was like music. These all involved the tempering process that gave the steel strength but removed the brittleness. Without it the steel could shatter like glass. I loved to see them quenched in the water, making the water boil around the hot metal and seeing the steam. Boys like violent reactions like fire or explosions.

I remember thinking it was common for kids like me to grow up in a great time and atmosphere like I was living. Only later in life did I realize I had come up in a fading time with the right people to give me unique experiences.

Sandpiper

The soft breeze shifts bringing the scent of brackish water to quavering nostrils.

Salt, oyster shells, and the wonderful smells where three waters of disparity come together. Inlet, bay, and waterway push and pull like struggling personas.

Strong fragrances of salt, fish, black sandy mud with tiny bits of shells, burnt diesel, and syrupy brown tannin from the trees. Large patches of reeds built up on mounds of mud and oyster shells, held in place by marsh grass and sea oats.

The oysters in their beds spit little streams as you pass by, beckoning, come closer. Little bearded bivalve's, mouths gaping, to say we will shred your flesh if you give us a chance, wooing, step closer into the slippery slimy mud.

Tiny crabs sit by their holes in the black goo. The fiddlers march carrying a violin, their songs are clicking, all the same pitch with no discernible harmony. They roll out tiny sand balls as expert excavators leaving hole for escape from man and fowl.

The little birds, sandpipers scurry around, their skinny twig like legs, moving faster than the eye can follow, putting one in front of the other, always moving forward never backing up making quick tight turns running from water, then chasing the bits of sustenance, as the foamed crooked line of surf pulls away.

Pausing to peck a speck too small to notice, her bony toes mark the mud writing in a cuneiform like language, a dead tongue not spoken for millennia. Beautiful shapes pointing, spelling out instruction and direction.

Lasting only seconds until the wind and water wipe the sand canvas clean. A new page is opened tempting and luring the small writer with tidbits of food, enticing her to write to live a little longer.

Shades of the Same Skin

Oregon

Adam Brown

From and currently resides: Oregon, USA

I was born to life of poverty, living on food stamps and section 8 housing with two mentally/physically disabled parents. I played all day and slept all night. I had a simple childhood filled with enormous amounts of fun.

Between watching movies with my Dad, playing my Nintendo, playing with friends, or getting on my mom's nerves, I had a little black covered book I would write short stories in. My mother and I would sing Freddy Fender and Johnny Cash and I absolutely adored the lyrics. It led me to listen to music constantly in my teens, which most likely influences my writing today.

I learned from my father at an early age to always root for the underdog, which is what led me to volunteer and intern with Oregon Student Public Interest Research Group while in college. I plan on changing the world one person at a time by helping out in the community, or just spilling my guts out in poetry (which hopefully inspires others to do the same.) I was born and live In Eugene, Oregon, United States.

Adam's pages:

www.AdamLevonBrown.com

www.ctupublishinggroup.com/adam-levon-brown-.html

The Slug

I grew up on 5th and Jefferson in the heart of Eugene, Oregon. I used to play outside a lot, sometimes with friends and sometimes alone. I was obsessed with spiders, ants, birds; anything that moved and lived.

One day, when I was 8 years old, I was out playing in the dirt in the yard next door to mine. It was a house that my friend Adrian lived in. We discovered a slug that appeared to be bleeding. I got really upset about it, picked it up gingerly with both hands and rushed home. I knelt down with the slug in my hands right outside of my family's apartment door.

> "MOM!" I yelled.

She is a stern woman and was born in Denison, Texas. She has a distinct accent.

> "Adam, did you warsh your face?" she asked.

Of course I didn't wash my face, only losers listen to their mom's, and I was cool kid.

> "Mommy, help. There is a hurt slug!" I yelled.

She smiled and handed me a can of abrasion healing spray. I immediately began spraying the slug down with spray only to find that it **killed the slug**.

I was so distraught that I started crying.

My dad is also stern, but gentler than my mom. He was born in Portland, Oregon and has a northwestern accent.

> "Adam, slugs don't use people medicine, it kills them," he said in a comforting voice.

I had tears streaming down my face and I was really quiet. My dad hugged me, but I will still crying for most of the day until it got dark. We laughed about it that night while watching television.

California fun

One hot and
Humid summer
Day in San Diego.

Surfboard in arm,
And a smile on my
Face.

Waves of blue-white
Foam splashing against
My bare, reddened ankles.

Feelings of joy
And carelessness
Overpowered
The insecurity
Which I held
Deep inside.

The Pacific
Warmed
The very blood
In my veins
And the hole
That had become
My heart.

I built
A sandcastle
That day
With my nihilism
As the sand

I let the waves
Of joy
Wash it
All away.

Shades of the Same Skin

Cultural Photo

This flower is a pink Rhododendron. They are native to Oregon and bloom early in the Spring time. I see them often on my hikes on Mount Pisgah and my walks through Delta Ponds here in Eugene.

Epilogue

Publishing Assistance

Starving Artist

In 2013 after publishing her own book, Ms. Raja Williams quickly realized that there were many writer's throughout the world needing assistance in getting published. Her writing peers were reaching out to her asking for assistance and guidance in getting their own work published. Many of the writers were from other countries indicating that even accessing the World Wide Web was a challenge for them, never mind trying to find a publisher to assist them. Financial hardships were also preventing writers from sharing their beautiful poetry and words of wisdom.

Right away Raja felt inclined to assist her writing peers so she established the "Starving Artist Fund." A fund that will assist writers that are ready to submit their manuscript and become published authors at either a discounted rate or a full publishing scholarship. In 2014 Raja published our first book "Love, A Four Letter Word" with the help from 28 poets from around the world that donated their work to the publishing of said book to help establish the startup fund. All proceeds from our sales from all anthology books are being donated to the Starving Artist Fund.

For More Information Please Visit Our Website At:

www.ctupublishinggroup.com/starving-artist-fund.html

Shades of the Same Skin

Creative Talents Unleashed

Get Connected With Us!

Website: Creative Talents Unleashed Publishing Group

www.ctupublishinggroup.com

Facebook: Get connected with us on our Facebook Page

www.Facebook.com/Creativetalentsunleashed

Twitter: https://twitter.com/CTUPublishing

Blog: www.creativetalentunleashed.com

Pinterest: https://www.pinterest.com/creativetalents/

Instagram: https://instagram.com/ctupublishinggroup/

Tumblr: http://creativetalentsunleashed.tumblr.com/

Book Credits

Book Cover – Donna J. Sanders

Creative Director – Donna J. Sanders

Editor – Donna J. Sanders

Publisher – Creative Talents Unleashed

<u>Royalty Free Photo Credits</u>

Pg. vi "World Hands"
https://pixabay.com/en/hands-world-map-global-earth-600497/

Pg. 1 "Around the World"
https://pixabay.com/en/world-map-earth-global-continents-146505/

Pg. 2 "Mexico"
https://pixabay.com/en/mexico-america-map-geography-146371/

Pg. 9 "Greece"
https://pixabay.com/en/map-greece-borders-country-1027679/

Pg. 16 "China"
https://pixabay.com/en/china-map-world-map-of-the-world-714768/

Pg. 23 "Africa"
https://pixabay.com/en/africa-map-gray-outline-306464/

Pg. 34 "India"
https://pixabay.com/en/india-map-world-map-of-the-world-714772/

Pg. 40 "Italy"
https://pixabay.com/en/italy-map-country-geography-153961/

Pg. 47 "England"
https://pixabay.com/en/united-kingdom-great-britain-black-303323/

Credits Continued

Pg. 55 "Caribbean Islands"
https://en.wikipedia.org/wiki/Portal:Caribbean/Map

Pg. 56 "Puerto Rico"
https://commons.wikimedia.org/wiki/File:Puerto-Rico-blank.svg

Pg. 63 "Jamaica"
https://commons.wikimedia.org/wiki/File:Jamaica_location_map.svg

Pg. 69 "Trinidad and Tobago"
https://en.wikipedia.org/wiki/Template:Location_map_Trinidad_and_Tobago

Pg. 75 "USA"
https://pixabay.com/en/map-usa-america-geography-united-835859/

Pg. 76 "Michigan"
https://pixabay.com/en/michigan-map-state-america-23565/

Pg. 80 "New York"
https://pixabay.com/en/map-new-york-state-geography-43774/

Pg. 85 "North Carolina"
https://pixabay.com/en/north-carolina-map-state-geography-43772/

Pg. 94 "Oregon"
https://pixabay.com/en/map-oregon-state-united-states-40179/

- All other photos content of Authors

Creative Talents Unleashed

Creative Talents Unleashed is an independent publishing group that offers writers an opportunity to share their writing talents with the world. We are committed to fostering and honoring the work of writers of all cultures. Our publishing group offers writing tips to assist writers in continued growth and learning, daily writing prompts and challenges to keep the writers mind sharp and challenged, marketing and events, as well as a variety of yearly publishing opportunities. We are honored to be assisting writers in the journey of becoming published authors.

www.ctupublishinggroup.com

For More Information Contact:

Creativetalentsunleashed@aol.com

www.ingramcontent.com/pod-product-compliance
Lightning Source LLC
Chambersburg PA
CBHW081015040426
42444CB00014B/3219